Contents

Education for Everyone

Y ou've probably heard a million times that school is important. It is. And not just because it can help you get your dream job one day. Education gives people power. It gives them the knowledge they need to make good decisions. It gives them a voice to demand that their governments do a better job. It gives them the confidence and the skills to change the world around them. Education is so important that the United Nations says it is a basic human right.

Missing Out

Unfortunately, just because education is considered a human right, that doesn't mean everyone gets to go to school. According to the children's charity UNICEF, there are more than 100 million children around the world who have never been to school.

Most of these children live in developing countries, where there isn't always enough money and resources to build schools. Even when there are schools, millions of children still miss out. In some cases, it's because their families live too far away from the schools, or because they can't afford to send the children to school instead of to work. In other cases, the children aren't allowed to go to school because of their gender, their background or where they come from.

And it's not just children in developing countries who get left behind. Children in developed countries live in all kinds of circumstances that can make it hard to go to school the traditional way. Some children live in remote places or in areas hit by natural disasters. Some have special physical needs. Others find it hard to learn in traditional classrooms following traditional lessons.

Finding the Answers

The good news is that many amazing people around the world aren't willing to sit back and let children miss out on an education. These people ask "What do we need to create so that these children, living here in these conditions, can learn?" And then, more importantly, they're answering the question by creating incredible schools like the ones in this book.

My
ool,
ur
rld

le and

Schools

Around the World

Susan Hughes

W

To Patrick and Michael Hughes, my sweet nephews

Franklin Watts
Published in Great Britain in 2016 by
The Watts Publishing Group

First published by Owlkids Books Inc. in 2011
10 Lower Spadina Avenue, Suite 400
Toronto, Ontario M5V 2Z2
www.owlkidsbooks.com

Text © 2011 and 2013 Susan Hughes

ISBN 978 1 4451 4959 2
Dewey number: 371

Printed in Malaysia

Franklin Watts
An imprint of
Hachette Children's Group
Part of The Watts Publishing Group
Carmelite House
50 Victoria Embankment
London EC4Y 0DZ

An Hachette UK Company
www.hachette.co.uk

www.franklinwatts.co.uk

Chapter One

Working with the Environment

All the things that we do and the places that we go, including the schools where we learn, are connected to Earth and its environment. Environmental problems such as climate change, severe storms, natural disasters and shortages of resources like energy and water can make it hard to build new schools, to get to them or to keep old schools standing.

More and more schools are teaching students how to reduce their impact on the planet. And more and more schools are being built to be environmentally sustainable. Sustainability is a way of building and living that meets people's needs now, while leaving enough resources (such as clean air and water) for people in the future. In a lot of cases, building sustainably also costs less money. And that goes a long way toward building more schools and getting more children off to school around the world.

Chalanbeel Region, Bangladesh

Boat Schools

Water, Water, Everywhere

In Bangladesh, students can miss months of school during monsoon season, when heavy rains cause floods. Even when schools are open, it can be impossible for students to get to them.

Climate change is making the flooding even more extreme by melting glaciers in the Himalaya Mountains. The runoff swells rivers and makes them overflow their banks. The floods damage farms, schools and other buildings. In the past few years, thousands of schools have been damaged, and hundreds have been destroyed completely.

Fact: The school boats (see p.9) are built locally using materials from the region. Many have flat bottoms so they can glide through shallow waters and over flooded land.

Floating Schools

After seeing many of his friends and family members in Bangladesh miss out on an education, an architect named Mohammed Rezwan decided he was not going to let floods stop any more children from getting to school. He decided that the best way to beat the rising waters is to rise with them – on a boat.

"I thought that if the children cannot come to the school, then the school should come to them," Rezwan explains. He raised enough money to open the first school boat in 2002. Now there are ninety boats that travel along a 250-kilometre stretch of rivers and streams in northwestern Bangladesh, giving thousands of children the chance to learn.

Ahoy (Class) Mates!

"Boat school is the combination of a school bus and schoolhouse," says Mohammed. Six days a week, each boat stops at different villages along the shore, picking up children who are mostly in the same year of school. When the classroom is full – about 30 to 35 students – the work begins.

For three hours, the students have lessons in maths, reading, writing, English, Bengali (the official language of Bangladesh), the environment and conservation. Then the boat returns all the students to their riverbank stops. From there, the boat moves on to pick up another set of students for another three-hour lesson. Each boat offers three sets of lessons a day.

The boats act as community centres, giving people the chance to learn about things like health care and new rice-farming methods.

Wireless Waves

Even though the boats float from place to place, they have electricity to run up to four computers, a printer, a DVD player and a CD player. Solar panels on the roofs provide all the electricity they need. The boats are connected to the Internet through wireless technology. Besides all the technology, the boats also stock hundreds of books.

ALL ABOARD
If it weren't for the boats coming to pick up the children at their "doorsteps", many young girls might not be going to school at all. Their parents wouldn't let them travel out of the village to the nearest government school because they believe the journey is dangerous. The journey also takes them away from home for too long. Now that the boat schools come to them, the girls have time to both learn and work.

Asia

Shey, India

Druk White Lotus School

A Spot of Green in the Desert

Students in Shey in the Ladakh region of India live high up in the Himalaya Mountains, in one of harshest environments on Earth – a high-altitude desert.

For half of the year or longer, severe winter weather closes the mountain roads and cuts off Ladakh from the rest of India. There are few resources and limited electricity. Ladakh is also prone to earthquakes. It doesn't sound like the easiest place to build a school, does it?

But the people of Ladakh had strong motivation for building a school. They were afraid that without a place to teach their children, they would lose their culture forever. Ladakh is unique in India, which is largely Hindu, because its people are mostly Buddhists of Tibetan descent.

Fact: To show the connection between the school, the community, and the world, the school's buildings are arranged in the circular shape of a religious symbol called a mandala. To Buddhists, the mandala represents the unity of all things.

Sustaining a Way of Life

The Druk White Lotus School was built to help sustain the Buddhist way of life in Ladakh. For centuries, the Ladakhi people's isolation protected their culture and their language (Bothi) from outside influences. Later, parents wanted their children to get an education, but there were few local schools. Children were sent away to boarding schools where they were taught in other languages and exposed to other cultures and values. It began to look like the traditional Ladakhi culture and way of life might be lost. The answer was to build a local school that blended Tibetan Buddhist culture with modern technology and learning, giving its students and their community the best of both worlds.

Sustaining the Environment

The lack of resources and electricity, combined with the Buddhist belief in doing no harm, shaped the school's sustainable design, construction and day-to-day operation. The school uses very little energy and creates little pollution. Solar panels provide all the school's electricity. The thick walls are designed to trap the Sun's heat and keep the school warm, even in the middle of winter. To avoid carrying materials over long distances, the school was built with local materials, including grass, timber, poplar wood and mud bricks. The granite walls were made from stones found on or near the site. The architects who designed the school also used some traditional building methods. After all, many hand-constructed buildings in the area have survived earthquakes and harsh weather for hundreds of years!

A solar-powered pump draws water from under the ground for drinking and washing.

The Druk White Lotus School has won several awards, including World Architecture Festival Awards for Best Green Building and Best Education Building.

The students learn traditional dances and songs and practise meditation. They are taught in both Bothi and English.

North America

South America

Xixuaú, Brazil

Rainforest School

Protecting the Amazon

My name is Mecias, and I am ten years old. I live in a village and go to school in the middle of the rainforest.

In my village, there are a few houses surrounded by the jungle, which has lots of animals and birds. We go fishing in canoes built by the people here in the village. There is a crocodile in the village port!

At my school there are nineteen children, ranging in age from four to sixteen years old. We all study in the same classroom. We have wireless Internet and a computer! We study mathematics, the Portuguese language, history, natural sciences and geography, and very often we talk about conservation.

We learn not to throw rubbish into the river, not to kill the animals and not to cut down trees unnecessarily. I like my class. My classmates, my teacher and I like being in the middle of the forest and breathing clean air.

Mecias lives in the remote village of Xixuaú, deep in the Brazilian rainforest. His village is on the banks of the Rio Negro river, and the only way to get there is by boat. To get to the closest city, Manaus, takes five days by canoe or thirty to forty hours by speedboat.

Until recently, Mecias' village was virtually cut off from the rest of the world. There was no electricity and no phones. Without electricity or a connection to the outside world, the villagers found it hard to earn a living without turning to illegal hunting, trapping or logging. The tiny one-room school offered only basic primary school, up to about Year 3 or 4. If students in the village wanted to go further in school, they had to move to Manaus.

A Window to the World

In 2002, everything changed. Working with a charity called the Solar Electric Light Fund (SELF), the villagers brought in solar panels, computers, a satellite system and wireless Internet equipment. They built a new school to house the panels and computer equipment. The Internet opened up a whole new world of possibilities for the school and its students. They could access Brazil's online learning programme, which gives them the chance to get a secondary education without having to leave their village. And they had access to a whole world of information, right in their classroom, without the need for expensive textbooks.

Today, the students in Xixuaú learn to work with computers, digital cameras and the Internet. They connect with schools and students around the world. Adults use the school in the evenings to take online classes. They also book eco-tours and run e-commerce businesses selling locally made crafts.

Fact: The Xixuaú–Xipariná Ecological Reserve is owned and run by the Caboclá, one of Brazil's native peoples. This untouched rainforest is home to countless plant and animal species.

Learning from the Forest

Chris Clark helped set up the school in Xixuaú, which has changed what and how it teaches over the years. He says, "The main challenges for the children were always the remoteness and the fact that the curriculum is invented in urban São Paulo, the largest city in Brazil. It bears no resemblance to their reality. Now our children create some of their own material. We are trying to create a more relevant curriculum, with subjects like forestry management, climate change and ecosystems."

The school has helped the community gain a whole new appreciation for the reserve (see above) and its importance in the world. And since families no longer have to move to the city for their children to finish school, they're able to stay on the reserve to help protect the forest they love.

Using solar power to access the Internet has shown the villagers of Xixuaú how much the rest of the world values the rainforest.

Canada

USA

Mexico

New Orleans, United States

Arthur Ashe Charter School

High Winds Bring High Hopes

On August 29, 2005, Hurricane Katrina ripped into the city of New Orleans with intense winds, pounding rain and a storm surge (sea level rise) 6.7 metres high. By the time the storm receded, 80 per cent of the city was flooded, more than 1,800 people had died and entire neighbourhoods were destroyed, including over one hundred schools.

Crisis = Opportunity

New Orleans was determined to come back stronger than ever after the storm. Katrina destroyed many schools that were old, crumbling and underfunded. The city took the opportunity to build stronger schools that would serve the students better. The new schools are designed to survive future storms, with roofs and windows that can withstand winds up to 210 kilometres per hour. They are built above the ground, so that they'll stay dry even if the city floods again.

But even more exciting is the fact that the schools aren't just protected from the environment. The schools and their students will be working to protect it.

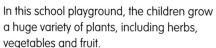

In this school playground, the children grow a huge variety of plants, including herbs, vegetables and fruit.

The Edible Playground

Imagine growing some of the food you eat right in your school playground. It would be cool to have such a close connection to what you eat, wouldn't it? That's something most students, especially those who live in the heart of a big city, never get the chance to experience. But students at a few schools in New Orleans, including the Arthur Ashe Charter School, are reconnecting with the land by getting their hands dirty. They have the chance to plant, grow and harvest organic fruit and vegetables; compost waste; and care for a wetland area and butterfly garden.

Students also learn about healthy and sustainable eating by cooking food from their garden and local farmers' markets in the Teaching Kitchen. As they munch on fresh, locally raised food, instead of food that is processed and shipped from far away, students experience first-hand how they can reduce their impact on the environment. Besides that, lessons have never tasted so good!

Fact: Hurricane Katrina forced about 372,000 students from the US states of Louisiana and Mississippi to leave their homes.

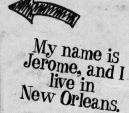

My name is Jerome, and I live in New Orleans.

I like the garden at Arthur Ashe. I help create a wetland area, and plant fruits and vegetables. I also help to dig flowerbeds and to weed them. I like it because after we finish growing the food, we can harvest it and eat it. Sometimes we can take it home. I've taken home aubergines, satsumas and onions. In New Orleans, we waste a lot of food. Also, people waste fuel because food is brought in from other states. If we all had gardens, we wouldn't have to ship in as much food.

Our school is moving into a new building. I like this school, but it is very old and small. The new school will be awesome. It will be good to have somewhere with grass where we can play. Also, the garden will be bigger. Not everyone gets a chance to work in the garden here. In the new school, more students will be able to learn about gardening and cooking.

New Ideas for Old Resources

Sometimes solving a seemingly impossible problem just takes a fresh way of thinking about it.

That was the case in Gando, Burkina Faso, where the village school was about to collapse in 1999. Without it, students would have to walk for hours to the closest school or stop going altogether. There was no money to repair the old concrete school, and building a new one seemed out of the question.

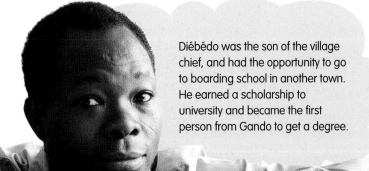

Diébédo was the son of the village chief, and had the opportunity to go to boarding school in another town. He earned a scholarship to university and became the first person from Gando to get a degree.

But not to Diébédo Kéré, an architect who grew up in Gando. He'd been studying architecture in Germany, and he believed that Gando had everything it needed to build a new school. It wouldn't be easy. The village had no electricity, few resources and no money to buy what was needed. But the biggest challenge would be convincing the villagers that clay – the one resource they had plenty of – could be used to build a sturdy school. The villagers had given up building with clay long ago because the rainy season damaged and destroyed clay buildings. They'd been building with expensive imported concrete for years, following designs brought in from places with cooler climates that weren't well suited to Gando's hot temperatures.

Cool Design

The old concrete-and-tin school was dark and hot inside. According to Diébédo, it was "like a room to bake bread, not to teach somebody." He wanted the new school to be comfortable – a place where students would want to be. Diébédo came up with ingenious ways to make the new school naturally bright and cool without air conditioning, fans or lights. His design was so impressive that it won awards around the world.

Build a Better School, Build a Better Life

With a lot of hard work, Diébédo made his dream of building a school to sustain his community a reality. Since 2001, Gando's villagers have built an addition to the school with a public library and teachers' housing. More than 800 students attend the school today. And with the new construction skills they learned building their school, Gando's villagers are earning money working on projects in other towns. Following Gando's lead, other communities are building sustainable schools and houses using clay bricks.

Fact: Diébédo designed an unusual roof for the school. It is raised off the ceiling, leaving a gap where hot air can escape from inside the school. It also allows cool breezes to blow in. The wide overhang helps shade the school from the Sun so it stays cooler.

The whole village of Gando helped build the school. Women stamped down the clay floor; children carried mud and stones; and men made the clay bricks, constructed the walls and put the roof in place.

The Gando villagers are mostly farmers, so Diébédo suggested putting a vegetable garden beside the school.

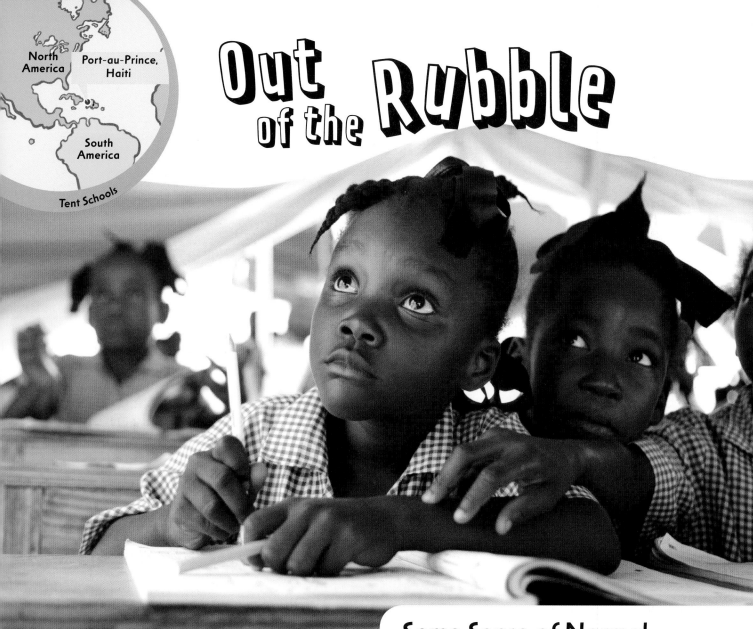

Out of the Rubble

North America

Port-au-Prince, Haiti

South America

Tent Schools

Some Sense of Normal

What if you woke up one morning and found that the world around you was completely different? That your house, your neighbourhood, your family and your friends were all gone?

That's what thousands of children in Haiti faced on 12 January 2010, when a powerful earthquake took their world and turned it upside down. The severe earthquake made buildings collapse as if they were made of cards. Streets disappeared under rubble. By the end of that day, more than 200,000 people had died. Life on the island slammed to a halt.

About half of the schools in and around the capital city, Port-au-Prince, were damaged or destroyed in the earthquake. Going to school, seeing friends and having a routine is really important for children after a disaster. It makes life feel closer to normal for a few hours a day.

But how do you get children back to school when the world around them is in chaos? When you can't even think about rebuilding until tons of debris have been cleared? You set up a temporary school, and you do it as fast as possible.

Tent Schools

In the days after the earthquake, charities such as UNICEF, Save the Children and Plan International helped schools that were damaged or destroyed set up tents so their students had somewhere to go for classes. They also set up tent schools near camps for people who had lost their homes. When it rained, the tent schools flooded and children had to go home. But on good days, the schools were full.

A Little Laughter

Knowing that the children were dealing with a lot of emotions, teachers wanted to make sure the tent schools were a fun and safe place. As well as having standard classes like reading, maths and French, they played games and sang songs with the children. Teachers also encouraged students to talk about their feelings so that they could start healing.

Fact: More than 1,400 schools were destroyed in the earthquake in Haiti.

SCHOOL-IN-A-BOX

UNICEF delivered hundreds of School-in-a-Box kits to Haiti. Each kit contains everything a teacher needs to set up a classroom. There is even a can of special paint that can be used to turn the box lid into a blackboard. Each kit has enough supplies for forty students to get back to school, at least temporarily.

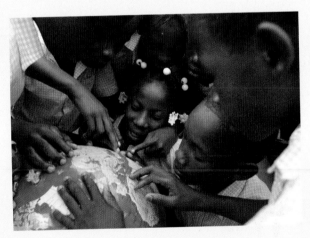

UNICEF sends the kits all over the world to help children get back to school after disasters like tsunamis and earthquakes. They also send kits to places where wars stop children from getting to school.

Canada

USA

Windsor, Canada

Dr. David Suzuki Public School

Every Day Is Earth Day

My name is Katarina. I am eleven years old, and I go to a "green" school.

My new school is an amazing learning experience. We learn about all the regular school subjects, such as maths and language, but we also learn about how to take care of the Earth properly. All of the teachers encourage us to use what we learn about taking care of the Earth everywhere we go.

My school has amazing eco-friendly technology. Another special feature is the statue of Dr David Suzuki in the main lobby of the school. It is a bronze sculpture of him as a young boy and a frog sitting on a large boulder. It shows that anyone can discover the Earth at any age.

This school has opened my mind more. I see the world in a new way. Everything seems so delicate, especially the environment. I'm now focused on saving this beautiful Earth we live on. At home, I always make sure to recycle. I also make sure every light is turned off when I'm getting ready for school.

When a world-famous environmentalist like Dr David Suzuki agrees to have a school named after him, you know it's going to be green. The Dr David Suzuki Public School in Windsor, Canada, isn't just eco-conscious – it's the most environmentally friendly school in the whole country. It's a model of sustainable design. And it's even more than all that. As the principal, Judy Wherry, says, it's a "teaching building". Because environmental awareness is built into the school and its culture, students learn to become "earth keepers", or stewards of the environment.

The outdoors comes indoors in the school library.

Fact: **Fact:** The school has the goal of eliminating rubbish. In fact, it doesn't even have bins. Every student gets a reusable water bottle and lunch bag so that they can bring litterless lunches. Food waste goes into composters in the school playground.

As they walk into school every day, students see the solar panels that provide some of their school's electricity.

Built-in Lessons

The school was designed to get students thinking about how the building and their use of it affects the environment. It was constructed in a way that allows students to see how the building functions, from its rainwater-collection system to its green energy sources. Transparent walls and windows let students see the geothermal heating and cooling systems and the solar-powered water heaters in action. Computer screens throughout the school show students how efficiently everything is operating.

Every part of the school has green features built in, even the roof. Half of it is covered with native plants to help insulate the building and reduce heat loss. The plants also provide a habitat for wildlife such as birds and insects. The roof has an outdoor classroom so students can do some of their learning outside.

Energy Efficient

The school was designed to reduce the amount of energy and water it uses. It uses two-thirds less energy than a normal building its size because it makes intelligent use of natural, non-polluting energy sources like the Sun. For instance, solar pipes allow sunlight to brighten the hallways and classrooms, while wind turbines and solar panels produce electricity to run the school. Geothermal heating and cooling systems use far less energy than air conditioning and gas-burning furnaces.

The school has a system for collecting and treating rainwater, which is used in the school's toilets and gardens. Two large cisterns buried under the school store enough rainwater to last 120 days.

Dr David Suzuki works tirelessly to promote sustainability and educate people about our impact on the planet. At the school's grand opening, he told the students, "All of you, in going through this school, you're going to come out a different kind of person. You are going to cause change that will ripple out far beyond the school."

Chapter Two

No School? No Way!

A lot of things can make it hard to get to school, from long distances to weather to natural disasters. But an even bigger hurdle than these physical barriers is one you can't see: people's attitudes. In some cases, people's beliefs keep a specific group of children out of school, whether it's girls or all children of a certain background or status. In other cases, children don't get the chance to go to school because no one seems to care if they go or not. These children slip through the cracks because they can't afford to pay for school, don't have a home address or aren't citizens of the country.

But there are schools and students trying to break down these barriers. They're embracing the idea that every child has a right to school, and they're finding inspiring ways to make that happen.

From Tip to Textbooks

One day in 2002, Phymean Noun had just finished eating lunch by the river in Phnom Penh, the capital of Cambodia. She threw away her chicken bones. Several children ran over and fought over them, licking them clean.

Phymean was shocked. "Why aren't you in school?" she asked. The children told her that they wanted to go to school, but their parents couldn't afford it.

Although public school is free in Cambodia, most teachers try to make students pay for their lessons because their salaries are low. Students must also have uniforms and school supplies. It all adds up to an expense that poor families just can't manage. These families also need their children to earn money.

Stung Mean Chey

More than 10,000 people live in a huge slum beside Phnom Penh's dump, Stung Mean Chey. Many of the adults and children who live in the slum work in the dump. They collect discarded items, such as aluminium cans, and sell them to recyclers. They earn the equivalent of about 64 pence a day.

24

A School Near Home

Phymean decided to create a school for these children right near the dump, close to where they lived. She says, "I decided to quit my job. I spent money from my savings on trying to get the school off the ground."

She set up the People Improvement Organization (PIO). She travelled to Canada, Australia, France and other countries, asking the Cambodian communities there for financial help. In 2004, Phymean opened the Stung Mean Chey Center next to the dump.

Food for Thought

The school offers free classes in English, Khmer (the official language of Cambodia), maths, social sciences and geography. It also provides students with free uniforms and school supplies, as well as health care. To help convince parents to let their children go to school instead of working, the school gives them free rice and some money every month.

The idea took off. There are now more than 200 students at the school. PIO has also opened the Borey Keila Center and the Borei Santipheap II Center in other poor areas of the city. The schools are the only options for children living there.

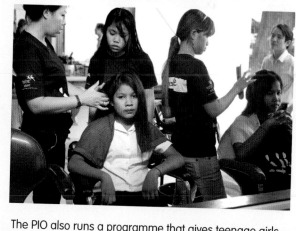

The PIO also runs a programme that gives teenage girls training to work in beauty salons. When the girls learn a trade, they have a better chance of getting a job, earning an income and giving back to their families and community.

Fact: More than 900 million people around the world live in slums.

Asia

Ramche, Nepal

Shree Santi School

A Chance for Change

My name is Sukra Bir Tamang. My school is in my village, high in the mountains of Nepal.

My village, Ramche, has a majority of Tamang people, a lower caste group. I feel proud being Tamang. I like my language, my culture and my community.

In our society in Nepal, there is discrimination because of the caste system. A Dalit – a member of the lowest caste – cannot enter a non-Dalit's house, which makes me sad. I don't like this thinking, as Miss Subhadra, our teacher, is a Dalit. I respect her.

There is discrimination in our society, but there is no discrimination in my school. I have many Dalit friends in my school. In social studies we learn to develop harmonious relationships among the people in our society. Plus, the teachers in my school teach us to treat all the people equally.

For thousands of years, there has been a caste system in Nepal. The highest caste groups are the wealthiest and have the most privileges. Lower caste groups do not have the same educational, political or social opportunities. They include Tamang people and Dalits. Dalits are considered "untouchable" under the caste system, and do not have any rights. They are excluded from Nepal's society in many ways.

Although the government has passed laws to create equality between all Nepalese people, the laws are hard to enforce. People's attitudes can take a long time to change, and discrimination still exists.

Fact: In Nepal, people of the lower caste groups, like the Dalits, face extreme prejudice. People shout insults at them as they walk down the street. They cannot enter temples or the homes of members of higher caste groups.

A School for Everyone

Nepal's government built schools near the villages of the higher caste groups, but not in the villages where mostly Tamangs and Dalits lived. Sukra's village hadn't had a school in years.

But a chance meeting on one of Nepal's city streets would change that. In 2003, an American tourist named Chris Heun met Lila Bahadur Tamang while backpacking, and the two became fast friends. Lila took Chris to visit his home village of Ramche. Chris was struck by the friendliness of the children he met there, and when he returned home he started fundraising to help build them a school.

It took several years, but the group, called the Santi School Project, finally raised enough money to start construction in 2008. When the school opened several months later, children from surrounding villages were eager to attend. Some walked for half an hour or more to get there! The school welcomed everyone, no matter their background. It also employed teachers of different castes. Two of the school's teachers are Tamang, one is Sherpa and one is Dalit. Chris Heun says, "One of our teachers, Subhadra, is the first and only Dalit woman in the village to stay in school past Year 11. Hopefully, many girls, especially minorities, will follow her example."

Fact: In 2007, the Nepalese government created a new constitution that promises a free education for every child. But it's a big promise to fulfill, and many children are still without a school.

With a Lot of Hard Work...

Because the village of Ramche is so remote, the designers decided to build the school entirely of local stone and wood. There are no roads into Ramche, so the materials had to be carried from the nearest town, 40 kilometres away.

The village had no electricity, so the villagers built the school by hand, using hammers, picks, handsaws, shovels and chisels.

Success!

The Shree Santi Primary School opened its doors in 2008 with five classrooms and a library. At first, only reception and Year 1 were offered. Now, more than seventy students attend the school's reception and Years 1 and 2.

The Promise of School

Imagine if the decision about who you would marry someday was made before you were born. And if, instead of going to school, you were married off at a young age to someone as old as your parents.

For girls in the Maasai society of Kenya, that's been a reality for centuries. Until 1999, that is, when Margery Kabuya came along with a plan to change their lives. She opened the Naning'oi Girls Boarding School, the first school for Maasai girls.

Booked for Marriage

Maasai fathers traditionally "book", or promise, their daughters for marriage when they are very young – sometimes before they are even born. In exchange, the fathers receive a dowry of several cattle, food and other gifts from the groom. This practice is called *Esaiyata*.

Fact: More than 80 million girls in developing countries will be married before they turn eighteen.

Exchanging Bridegrooms for Classrooms

Esaiyata is an important age-old custom in the Maasai culture. Margery knew that she'd never get parents to send their girls to school if she tried to stop *Esaiyata*. Instead, she incorporated the practice into her approach. With the help of a well-respected community leader, Chief Simeon Keshoko, she recruited several Maasai elders to act as "suitors" for the school.

The suitors approach girls' fathers, offering them a dowry of cattle, food and other gifts. Instead of booking the girls for marriage, they book them for school. The girls are enrolled for eight years at Naning'oi, and their fathers promise not to marry them off during that time. The girls live full time at the school.

When girls are already booked for marriage, their fathers and future husbands are offered a dowry refund to allow them to go to school. Chief Keshoko encourages people in the community to contribute the cattle, goats and sheep needed for dowry refunds. He has helped convince many adults that education for girls is good for the whole community.

The Commitment Grows

The first year, four girls began studying at the Naning'oi Girls Boarding School. Since then, over 350 students have attended the school, and 500 more are booked.

Esaiyata is a serious bond, and all the parents who agree to send their girls to school honour their promise not to marry them off during that time. Almost 100 per cent of the students finish the eight years of school.

Some will return home after primary school to get married. Others want to postpone marriage and continue their education, if their families are willing and can afford to pay.

The school has six classrooms, nine teachers and a house where the girls live and sleep. It is funded by ChildFund International, an organisation that sponsors children around the world.

Fact: Educating girls helps entire communities in a number of ways. An educated girl grows up to be an educated woman and mother. She's more likely to be:
- better paid in the workplace
- healthy and well nourished
- active in politics and community life
- able to send her own children to school.

29

Small School, Big Changes

Europe
Asia
Africa
Kalou, Iran

Shahid Rajaei Elementary School

The building for Abdul-Muhammad's school was donated to the people of Kalou.

The remote fishing village of Kalou, near the Persian Gulf in Iran, is so small that it doesn't appear on satellite maps of the Earth. Its school has just four students. But thanks to a blog about the village and its tiny school, life changed almost overnight for kids in Kalou, especially the girls.

Kalou didn't even have a school before 2008, when a teacher named Abdul-Muhammad She'rani arrived with the goal of setting one up. The village let him use a fishing shed, and on the first day of school, he and the students cleaned it out and set up a classroom inside.

Putting Kalou on the Map

Abdul-Muhammad was so excited about the new school, called Shahid Rajaei, that he started a blog about it. He described the students' enthusiasm, as well as the limited supplies and space he had to work with. In one entry, he called his school the smallest in Iran. News channels picked up the story of his tiny school, and it caught the attention of people all over the world. UNESCO named it "the World's Smallest School".

People began sending letters, money, textbooks and other gifts. Someone paid for the village to build a brand new schoolhouse. The government sent new desks and a computer. Almost overnight, the kids in Kalou had gone from having no school to having one of the most famous schools in the world.

> **Fact:** UNICEF estimates that around the world more girls than boys are missing out on school. How many girls is that? About 60 million.

Shahid Rajaei Elementary School

Hamideh (left and centre) is working hard to go further in school than any girl in her village has. She often does homework on the beach.

Changing Minds & Lives

All this attention had a big effect on the life of the school's oldest female student, Hamideh. After finishing at Shahid Rajaei in 2009, Hamideh started going to secondary school in a city 40 kilometres away. That would have been unthinkable just a few years earlier.

Hamideh's father had not planned for Hamideh to continue her education past primary school. Most parents in the village thought that girls did not need to go further in school. They also did not want their daughters moving to the city, which was the only option if they wanted to continue their studies.

Abdul-Muhammad says, "It was our tiny school and the many visitors it drew to Kalou that made Hamideh's father change his mind. Since the school got famous worldwide, he realised that Hamideh would benefit from continuing her education. Hamideh was breaking tradition to do so."

Once Hamideh's father agreed, Abdul-Muhammad convinced the government to set up a school bus route to drive Hamideh to secondary school and back every day. That way, she didn't have to move to the city. And now that the village has a school bus stop, younger girls will be able to continue their education when they finish at Shahid Rajaei – just like Hamideh!

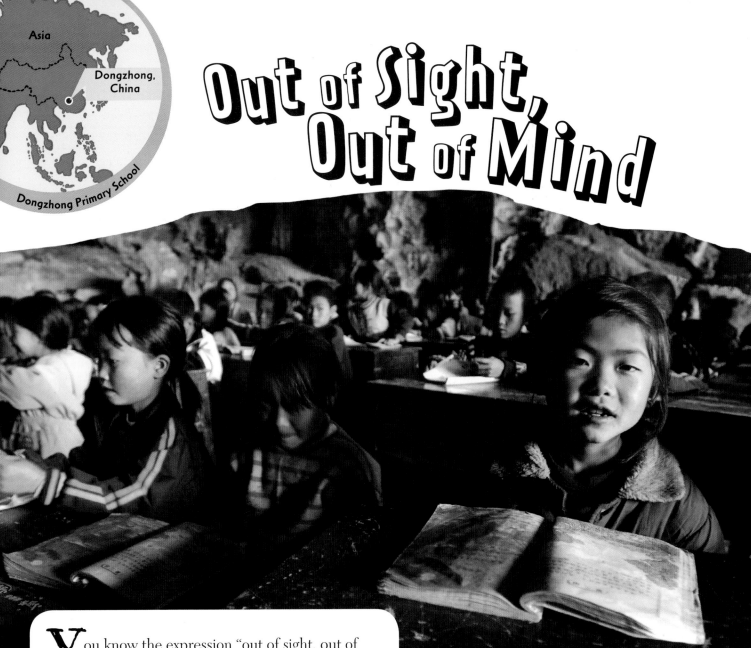

Asia

Dongzhong, China

Dongzhong Primary School

Out of Sight, Out of Mind

Y ou know the expression "out of sight, out of mind"? People sometimes use it to explain why they've forgotten something. Sadly, that expression can be used just as easily for people as it is for homework or keys. It's why some people fall through the cracks and no one seems to notice.

This is what happened to an entire village of people in southwest China. The village, called Dongzhong, is made up of Miao people, who are one of China's ethnic minority groups. They lived in almost complete isolation in the mountains, and they were all but forgotten by China's government. The families struggled to run a village school by themselves.

It was almost impossible to get teachers to move to Dongzhong, where there was no electricity, running water or heating. There was almost no money, either. The school had one teacher, offered only Years 1 and 2, and had few books or supplies. Students could barely read and write by the time they finished school.

Fact: Most of the children who miss out on primary school around the world live in rural areas.

School in a Cave

Dongzhong and its school were a bit unusual. Both the village and the school were inside a cave! The villagers are the last known people in China to live in a cave all year round.

Into the Spotlight

Dongzhong's unique location caught the attention of a television producer, who featured it on a show in China. As soon the show aired, things began to change for Dongzhong. Viewers were amazed by the villagers and were impressed by the students' eagerness to learn. They wanted to give them the chance to get an education.

Volunteers came to teach, and people across China began donating money, food, desks, art supplies, sports equipment, musical instruments and other school supplies. A businessman paid to have electricity lines run up the side of the mountain to the cave. The government began providing the village with free electricity.

Soon, the school had eight teachers and taught students up to Year 4. There were almost 200 students, many coming from neighbouring villages. Most walked between one and three hours each way, but some students lived at the school.

A Typical Day

Aside from the bats and birds flying over students' heads, a school day at Dongzhong Primary School was pretty typical. Students learned art, music, maths and Mandarin, which is China's official language. They are the first in their village to learn Mandarin. The older villagers speak only the Miao language, and most cannot read or write.

In 2011, all the attention that made the school successful led to its closure. The government said that the cave school's publicity was making education in China look "backward". It shut down the school and built a new, more traditional one nearby.

Students worked hard before and after school. Most took their family cows out to pastures on the mountainside and returned home late in the evening. Students from other villages who were staying at the school gathered water and firewood to cook their own supper over the firepits.

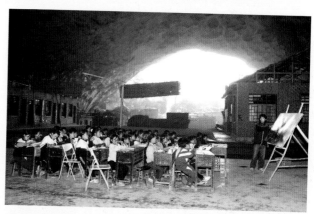

The cave school had a built-in floor and roof. The walls were made of woven bamboo that grows nearby.

The school is gone, but inside the cave there are still houses, livestock pens and small shops. There are also a few TVs, DVD players, satellite dishes and mobile phones.

Africa — Mutundwe, Uganda

ABC School

ABC Is for Everyone

My name is Anita, and I am eleven years old. I live at ABC School.

My previous school was a day school only. I was travelling by foot from home to school every day. I had to start walking at 5:30 in the morning to be there by 7:30.

I used to get so tired. I would have to wake up when I still wanted to sleep. I would leave school tired and go home, and then I would start cleaning the house, washing the utensils and sweeping. My father decided I should go to boarding school because my stepmother was giving me too much to do. He knew I would have time to concentrate on my studies if I came here. Also, the school performs well at national examinations. My father wants me to be a lawyer. That's what I want, too!

Now life is just better! After classes I just bathe, relax and play a little. I do my homework after eating dinner, and at 9:00 pm all of us are in bed.

My neighbours at home do not go to school. They used to go to school, when their father was still alive, but when he died they stopped going to school. Some people say he died of HIV/AIDS.

How many students are in your class? Imagine having more than a hundred classmates. That wouldn't be easy, would it? But that's what students in many schools around the world have to deal with, because there just isn't enough money, room or resources.

It's like that in Uganda. Classes with a hundred students are common, and there aren't enough books and other supplies to go around. In 1996, Uganda's government stopped charging fees for public schools. Almost overnight, schools were flooded with more students than they could handle. Today, Uganda still does not have enough public primary schools for everyone. Private schools offer better conditions, but for many families, it's impossible to pay the fees.

Fact: An international foundation helps ABC School raise money for new classrooms, books, teachers' salaries and food and housing for the students. It also sponsors children whose parents have died from AIDS, so they can live at the school for free.

Students at ABC School eat a food called posho made from maize flour and beans.

We Can Do Better

In 2004, teacher Hanan Bulime decided the children in his village of Mutundwe needed a better option than the closest public school. The school was far away, so students had to walk for hours every day if they wanted to attend. Plus, with overcrowded classrooms and few supplies, the school couldn't give students the kind of education Hanan felt they deserved.

Two weeks before the school year was supposed to begin, Hanan set up a desk under a tree in his village and hung a sign that said he was accepting registrations for his school – a school that didn't actually exist yet. There was no building, no desks and no books. But Hanan wasn't worried. And he wasn't surprised when forty students signed up within a couple of days. He quickly hired two more teachers, and soon there were three classes of students having lessons under a tree. ABC School was born.

Board by Board, Bit by Bit

Hanan convinced a villager to lend the school some land with a small brick building on it. But there were already too many students to fit inside!

When others in the village heard this, they pitched in and gave Hanan bamboo, boards and tin. With the help of some villagers and several students, he soon built a new classroom. More classrooms were added as more students joined the school.

Today, more than 400 students attend the school. Many of these students are AIDS orphans who attend the school for free. They have the chance at an education they might not be able to afford otherwise.

North America

Tegucigalpa, Honduras

South America

El Hogar de Amor y Esperanza

Off the Streets, Into School

My name is Yordi, and I'm thirteen years old. I live in the city of Tegucigalpa, Honduras.

Eight years ago, my mother died. There was only my grandmother to care for me. Sometimes she worked, and sometimes she couldn't find work. We were living in a mud house with no windows, no electricity and no water. I couldn't go to school because we couldn't pay for it.

Then, three years ago, my grandmother died. I didn't have anyone to take care of me. Luckily, a friend of my mother's knew about El Hogar de Amor y Esperanza, which means the Home of Love and Hope. I came to live here. It is very special because it is an orphanage for boys and girls, and at the same time it is a school.

This year, because I'm older, I started going to school at the technical school. I live there, too. I am finishing my first year of carpentry. When I've finished the course, I'd like to go to university and study to be a civil engineer! I want to get a good job and get married.

It is a huge blessing for me to be here. If I hadn't come here, I know I would be on the street, without any opportunities. There are a lot of gun groups in our city because there are many, many children who didn't have the opportunities that I have.

Yordi lives in Honduras, one of the poorest countries in the Western world. Thirty percent of workers are unemployed. Many fathers have to leave their families to find work in other countries. About half of families are made up of mothers struggling to raise their children alone.

Finding a Place

Half the people living in Honduras are children under eighteen, and hundreds of thousands of them are living on their own. Wanting to belong somewhere, about 100,000 kids have joined gangs. Yordi's school, El Hogar, was created to give kids an option besides gangs.

EL HOGAR DE AMOR Y ESPERANZA

Home and School

El Hogar is home to 260 students. Some of the students are orphans. Others have been abandoned. All of them live and study at the school for free. They also receive medical care. The school runs on donations from people living in North America.

Into the Working World

El Hogar goes up to Year 7. But the learning doesn't stop there! The school's goal is to help students become active citizens, so they don't return to the streets when they finish school. When students finish Year 7, they move on to one of El Hogar's secondary schools. They can choose the technical school, where they learn trades such as carpentry or welding or the agricultural school, where they learn new farming methods. When they finish secondary school, students are ready to head out into their communities and share their learning.

When the children at El Hogar aren't in lessons, they play football and basketball, draw with chalk and play games like marbles. This is often a whole new experience for them.

Because there are ten times more boys than girls on the streets, the school at first only took boys. Now El Hogar is home to a few girls as well.

Fact: About 143 million orphaned kids live in developing countries.

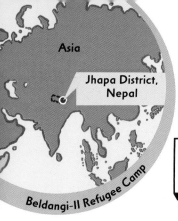

Asia

Jhapa District, Nepal

Beldangi-II Refugee Camp

Building Hope in a Refugee Camp

Fact: The UN estimates that there are more than 11 million refugees in the world. Tens of thousands of refugees live in camps in Nepal.

Imagine having to flee your home, taking only what you can carry, to move to a foreign country where you have no home, no school and no rights. You would end up in a refugee camp with hundreds or even thousands of people like you, living in tents and waiting to see where you could go next. That's the situation millions of people face every year to escape violence or war in their countries.

For refugees, school offers hope. It leads to a future outside of the camps. But many host countries do not allow refugees to attend their schools. It is up to refugees to set up and run their own schools for their children.

That was the case in Nepal, where refugees fled to escape violence in Bhutan. In one camp, Beldangi-II, they had few resources but a lot of determination. Teachers offered to work for little or no pay. Some parents built and maintained the classrooms, while others ran the schools or worked with the UN and other groups to get supplies and donations. Together, they built a successful school system. Although the schools are often short on supplies, the students manage to excel. More than 90 per cent of students pass their national exams in secondary school, which means they can go on to college or university in Nepal.

In Beldangi-II camp, the refugees are not allowed to build permanent buildings so they make their own huts out of bamboo.

Fact: Most of the textbooks for the lower years are made by the refugees themselves. Refugees write their own books, pull together material from several existing books or translate other books.

My name is Madan Kumar Giri. I was born in Bhutan.

Life in Bhutan was terrible for us because of my family's background. We are of Nepalese descent. We did not enjoy any kind of rights in Bhutan.

We went to live in a refugee camp in the eastern part of Nepal. It was called Beldangi-II. None of the refugees were allowed to work. Most adults played cards throughout the day. The women did the housework. I had to wait two years in the camp before a school opened.

When I was eight, I started to go to a school about ten minutes away from our hut. There were 14,000 students in our school! The classrooms were very congested and dusty.

My school was made of bamboo and thatch. I used to sit on a handmade carpet on the ground with my friends. When we reached Year 10, we got desks and benches. We had books, papers and pens supplied by a relief organisation called Caritas Nepal. There was no electricity in the camp or in our schools. We studied subjects like maths, science, social studies, English, Nepali and Dzongkha, the national language of Bhutan.

After seventeen years in the camp, my family and I immigrated to Canada. The best thing about school was that we were taught in English. It is really helpful to me now!

Chapter Three

One Size Doesn't Fit All

If your school is like most others, you probably have a set schedule with set classes. You are expected to be in a certain place at a certain time, five days a week. For most students, this traditional approach to learning works fine.

But that doesn't mean it works for everyone. Some students learn better outside classrooms, in non-traditional ways. Some children have families that are always on the move, so they have to choose between travelling or staying put to go to school. Other children have to choose between going to school or working to earn money. And when those children don't know where their next meal will come from, it's not really a choice at all. They have to work to survive.

The thing all these children have in common is this: they need schools to be flexible. Fortunately, some creative people are working hard to make this happen. The result? More incredible and unusual schools – and even more children heading off to learn!

Evenk Nomadic School

A School on the Move

The Evenk school (see p. 43) teaches a total of 23 six- to ten-year-old children living in several different camps.

What if going to school meant leaving your family for months at a time, starting when you were six years old? And learning a completely new language? It might be hard being away from your family for so long. And it might be difficult to hold on to the life and culture you left behind. That was the situation Evenk children faced for decades.

The Evenks are one of Siberia's indigenous (native) peoples. Their lifestyle is based on raising reindeer. They move their herds over a huge territory of more than 1,500 square kilometres, from one grazing area to the next. Several families live in a camp and travel together. For centuries, Evenk children learned from their parents and elders everything they needed to know in order to continue their way of life as reindeer herders.

But in the late 1960s, the Soviet government passed a law saying that all children had to attend school and follow a standard set of courses. Because their families were nomadic, the Evenk children had to leave them behind and board at the state schools. That meant they were away from their families and communities for months at a time. Evenk children began losing touch with their traditional way of life, including their language.

Protecting a Culture

In 1994, a young Frenchwoman named Alexandra Lavrillier arrived as part of an expedition to photograph Siberia's indigenous peoples. She was impressed by the Evenk people's warmth and the fact that they had preserved their culture in spite of the challenges. But she knew that the only way to really protect their culture was to create a school just for the Evenk children. It took several years, but Alexandra finally got permission from the Russian education ministry to begin her "experimental school" in 2006. Alexandra's dedication to the school earned her the Rolex Award for Enterprise in 2006.

From Camp to Camp

Knowing how difficult it would be for Evenk children to go to one central school, Alexandra set up the school to go to the children instead. Many of the teachers are of Evenk descent, and they travel by sledge from camp to camp, bringing the school with them. Lessons are held inside a tent, where there is a computer powered by a generator. The amount of time the teachers spend at each camp depends on the number of students and their level of learning.

The school's curriculum reflects the belief that the students need to learn how to deal with the modern world in order to protect their rights. So besides the Russian curriculum, the students also learn English, French and how to use the Internet.

Sharing the Traditions

The Evenk children also learn about their heritage. As they do, they are helping with a project to create handbooks about the Evenk language, culture and traditions. Some of these books will also share the Evenk people's knowledge of local plants and animals and the environment. They will describe the Evenks' traditional way of life and explain how they manage their resources. The books will help other non-nomadic Evenks, who are living in towns and cities, stay connected to their roots.

When the teachers pack up and leave for the next camp, the Evenk children stay behind with their families. They study and do homework to prepare for their teachers' return, and they also spend time learning traditional skills, such as hunting, fishing, gathering berries and caring for reindeer.

Fact: Nomadic peoples live in many countries throughout the world. Many are indigenous peoples who continue to live their traditional lifestyle.

The Portable Schools Project

Have you ever heard of a Take Your Child to Work Day? Maybe you've even been part of one. It's a cool idea. Children take a break from school and find out what adults do all day. But what if every day was Take Your Child to Work Day because you weren't allowed to go to school? And the workplace you had to go to with your parents was a dangerous construction site? That's what life was like for the children of migrant workers in Thailand. But then a professor named Graeme Bristol and his architecture students in Bangkok came up with a brilliant solution – the Portable Schools Project.

FACT: It's impossible to know the exact number of undocumented migrant workers in the world, but the International Organization for Migration estimates there were about 30 to 40 million in 2005.

Migrant Workers

Thailand is home to thousands of undocumented migrant workers from neighbouring Burma, Cambodia and Laos. These people don't have official paperwork giving them permission to live and work in Thailand, so they usually take on dangerous, low-paying jobs no one else wants. Many work in construction. When the work is finished at one jobsite, they move on to the next one.

Students Helping Students

Graeme knew that many of the migrant workers' children were not permitted to go to Thai schools. He wanted to build a school just for them. But it wasn't practical to build a permanent school for families who would be moving on as soon as the work at their jobsite was finished. So Graeme decided to give his senior architecture students a challenge: design and build a portable school that could move easily from jobsite to jobsite with the workers' children.

First, Graeme's students interviewed the workers to see if they would value and use a school. They asked the children what they wanted their school to be like. They looked at schools in the area to see what might suit the needs of the children. Then they began designing.

The first portable school, which also operates as a nursery, opened in 2009. Instead of going to the construction site with their parents, the children go to nursery and school.

Made of Bamboo

The architecture students created a school made up of floor, wall and roof panels that attach quickly and easily to a frame. The panels and frame are made of lightweight bamboo, which grows locally. They can be taken down, moved and reassembled in a new location.

However, the first school Graeme and his students built was so popular, it may never be moved!

Kone, New Caledonia

Australia

New Zealand

Alberta Distance Learning Centre

Going to School Half a World Away

My name is Laura, and I am eleven years old. I live in one place, and I go to school somewhere else!

I live in New Caledonia, which is a tiny island between New Zealand and Australia, but I go to school in Canada.

I came here from Canada when I was ten. My family decided to move because my father was offered a job promotion at a nickel mine here. We really made the big decision to move because I think we all just couldn't resist the adventure of moving to a place we'd never go to otherwise. We'll be here for two years.

My teachers are in Canada. They work with the Alberta Distance Learning Centre. We communicate by email. When I finish my assignments, I send them by email to my teachers. They help me with my work and mark it. They email it back corrected and marked.

School begins for my brother and sister and me at nine o'clock. Depending on what day it is, I do two different subjects, one in the morning and one in the afternoon. I have only four subjects: social studies, maths, language and science. I do my schoolwork at home, sitting at my computer desk.

The thing I like best about virtual schooling is that I am able to learn so much and enjoy it. I can concentrate better, and my marks are much higher than when I lived in Canada. It's also taught me self-discipline, because there is nobody telling me what to do. I have to get my schoolwork done without the encouragement of a teacher. But sometimes I miss having classmates.

Canadian students like Laura have been able to learn long-distance for decades, although they didn't always do it through email.

In the 1940s, the children of trappers, loggers and railway workers lived in tiny remote settlements across Canada. The communities were too small to have permanent schools and teachers. So in some cases, school came to the students. Eight railway carriages were set up as classrooms, and trains pulled these carriages from one remote community to another. When the school pulled into the station, students would make their way there by canoe, on foot or by rail handcars.

Marks by Email

Canada still has many very small, very remote communities, especially in the Far North. Children living in these communities often do their learning at home. The provinces of Alberta, British Columbia and Saskatchewan run distance-learning centres to reach students who live too far from their nearest school to attend in person.

In the past, teachers sent their students books and assignments through the post – sometimes by bushplane! The students would complete their lessons, then post them back to their teacher. If students had questions, they would have to write letters to their teacher and wait for a response – sometimes for weeks.

Today, most of the schoolwork goes back and forth through email. That allows Canadian students like Laura to live just about anywhere in the world but still "go" to school in Canada.

Laura says, "I think this type of school would be difficult for some people. Really outgoing people would probably find it boring. For some people, having classmates is what motivates them to do well in school."

Cali and Popayán, Colombia

South America

Mobile Schools

Taking It to the Streets

Arnoud Raskin with some of the children he has helped.

How do children and young people end up living on the streets? Why do they sometimes choose to stay there? What would it take to get them to school? These are some questions that Arnoud Raskin wrestled with during his last year of university in Belgium. He wasn't studying to be a social worker or a teacher, though. Arnoud was studying to become a product designer. His final project at university was to design and make a new product. But Arnoud didn't want to design yet another thing for people to buy. Instead, he wanted to design something that could help change the lives of the young people who need it the most – street kids.

A Student of the Streets

To design a good product, Arnoud knew he needed to learn as much as he could about the people he was creating it for. He flew to Cartagena, Colombia, to volunteer with a group that worked with street kids. After spending months with the group, he realised that the biggest challenge in the kids' lives wasn't finding food and shelter. They were good at surviving on the streets. The biggest challenge was that they had been treated as worthless for so many years that they didn't believe they could have a better life. They didn't think they deserved it. Arnoud had found his inspiration. He would design something that helped street kids to see their great potential.

The Mobile School's lessons are based on listening to the children, encouraging them to believe they are important and giving them the information to make good choices for themselves.

Going to the Kids

Arnoud knew that programmes trying to get street kids into schools hadn't worked. So he decided to try something different – getting a school onto the streets. He designed a cart that contains everything a street teacher needs to set up school on the pavement.

Teaching the Basics and More

The cart is made up of a box with panels that slide out like a telescope. Each cart has 250 different activities. The street teachers decide which activities to do each day, depending on who turns up for classes. There are activities for teaching maths, health, telling the time and reading. The teachers also pass on a lot of important information to the students about healthcare and community services. Most of the activities are set up as games so that learning is fun and relaxed. The students also have chances to express themselves through puppetry and other creative outlets. It helps them deal with the sad and scary things that may have happened in their lives.

A busy Mobile School in Venezuela.

Asia

Pune and Mumbai, India

Door Step School

Schools That Go to Kids

I ndia has more street kids – about 18 million – than any other country. In India's big cities, a lot of obstacles can get between these children and school. When they don't have an official address, children can't register at a school. Some live in slums that are far from schools and they have no way to get back and forth every day. India also has millions of child workers. Instead of going to school, these children have to go to work. Other children miss out on school because they have to take care of their brothers and sisters while their parents work.

So what kind of school could work for all these children? One that comes right to their doorstep. In fact, Door Step School is the name of a group that brings classes to children across Mumbai and Pune, two of India's biggest cities. The group runs three buses, known as a School-on-Wheels, that give the term "school bus" a whole new meaning!

Fact: About 215 million children around the world have to work instead of going to school.

School-on-Wheels

Two School-on-Wheels buses operate throughout Mumbai, and one drives around Pune. Every day, the buses drive certain routes, stopping at specific spots so the children in that neighbourhood always know when to expect them. The buses spend about two or three hours at each spot, and children are free to come and go when they can.

The inside of each bus is set up as a classroom. The seats have been removed to make room for a blackboard and cabinets filled with books, art supplies, toys and other learning equipment. Up to 25 children can fit inside at once. Students work at their own pace, with help from the teacher. They learn reading, writing, maths, social science, science and art. They also learn about hygiene, health, safety and computers.

Field Trips

With a bus for a school, the School-on-Wheels takes the students to visit places like museums, hospitals, banks and police stations. Through these trips, the students begin to feel included in the life of their city, and they learn about the social services that are available to them.

Besides running the School-on-Wheels programme, the Door Step School helps students gain admission to their local school to get a formal education. The programme also offers students a lift to and from school.

Fact: The Indian government promises education for all children between the ages of six and fourteen. That's a big challenge – India is home to almost half a billion children!

The Door Step School was founded in 1988. Since then, over 50,000 children have been taught at more than 125 locations in Pune and Mumbai.

A Sense of Independence

Europe
Asia
Glasgow, United Kingdom
Africa
Hazelwood School

If your school is like most, it has a lot of stairs, hard surfaces and long, straight hallways with echoing walls. These features make it harder for students who have hearing or visual impairments to get around. For students who also have developmental or mobility impairments, it might just make it impossible. However, Hazelwood School, in Glasgow, Scotland, was built especially with these students in mind.

Outside the Box

Increased independence is the goal for Hazelwood's students, so they needed a school that would help them get around on their own. For example, many students use wheelchairs or walking frames, so there could be no stairs to get in their way.

The architects designing the school did everything they could to understand the needs of the children and young people who would be using it. They spoke to students, parents, teachers and other experts to get ideas. They even spent time wearing sight inhibitors at a school to try to experience the world as many of the Hazelwood students do.

In the end, they designed a softly curving building with built-in visual, tactile (touch) and sound cues to help students find their way around. For instance, there are high ceilings in the hallway that gradually become lower near classrooms. Students know they are nearing a classroom because the lower ceiling changes the sound of their footsteps. Classroom doors have the room name in Braille and in Moon tactile text, which is a text created for people who are blind and have learning difficulties. Different areas of the school are made of materials with distinctly different textures, including cork, stone and wood. These textures allow students to feel when they are moving from one part of the school to another.

FACT: About 150 million children around the world live with disabilities.

FACT: People with multiple sensory impairments have some degree of both blindness and deafness.

Hazelwood School for Children and Young People with Sensory Impairment opened in 2007. It can take up to sixty students per year. Part of helping the students be independent is teaching them life skills, so the school has cooking and computer rooms. It also has a three-bedroom life skills house on campus, where some students stay in residence. The school also has a music room, an art room, physiotherapy rooms and outdoor play areas with special bikes, swings and tunnels.

Asia

Bhubaneswar, India

Train Platform Schools

A Step Up with Platform Schools

Back in 1985, Inderjit Khurana, a successful teacher in Bhubaneswar, India, noticed what thousands tried to ignore as they hurried to and from work on the trains every day: hundred of children living, working and trying to survive in and around the station. They were begging, picking through rubbish, selling tea, polishing shoes – anything they could do to earn a bit of money.

Inderjit wanted to reach out to the children. She felt that they were missing out on their childhood. To bring them a bit of fun, she started reading stories on the platform. At first, most of the children were suspicious. They weren't used to a well-dressed person paying them so much attention.

But over time, Inderjit won their trust, and the storybook sessions evolved into a school, held every week on the platform. The children wanted to learn to read the stories for themselves. Soon, they were asking to have classes every day. At first, Inderjit's platform school had eleven students. Today, her group runs twelve platform schools, as well as job training for older students.

Fact: The Ruchika Social Services Organisation (RSSO) that Inderjit Khurana founded helps more than 6,000 students.

Zero Barriers to School

Every morning when the rush hour ends at around seven or eight o'clock, the train platforms are empty. The children have to wait for hours for them to fill up again. It's the perfect time for teachers to set up their platform schools. They carry books, toys, pencils and other materials to their corners of the platforms. Then they draw chalk lines on the ground to mark off the school from the rest of the platform.

The lack of walls is part of Inderjit's belief that there can be "zero barriers" to school for these children. The students are welcome to come and go as they please, and to bring younger brothers and sisters along. The schools hold classes in the mornings, leaving the children free for the rest of the day. The school day ends at eleven o'clock, when the teachers give all the students lunch.

Make It Fun and Children Will Come

The teachers know that they have to compete with a lot of other things in order to get the children to come to school. So they make learning fun. They use singing, dancing, puppet shows and other entertaining activities to teach the students basic maths, reading, writing and health.

Their goal is to bring some laughter into the children's lives, while helping them catch up with children going to traditional schools. When students are ready, RSSO helps them get into one of these schools. The group pays the school fees and buys uniforms and other things the students need.

The platform schools use activities like puppet shows to teach students basic skills, including maths and reading.

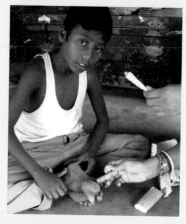

Every Saturday, students wash using jugs of water and soap. Doctors also come regularly to check up on them.

Canada

USA

Paris, United States

Grand Oaks Academy

The "Unschool" in a Tree House

Have you ever dreamed about not having to go to school? Or about how great it would be to tell your teacher what you wanted to learn, instead of the other way around? That's what children and families are doing in countries around the world. It's a movement known as "unschooling". Instead of going to their local school, the children learn at home, in their local libraries and in their community. They follow a plan that they help design with their parents or educators. Or they might learn without following any plan at all!

Erin and Jessica Stevens, who live in Tennessee, in the United States, may go to a normal school now, but they got ready for it first by staying out of school.

From Homeschooling to Unschooling

When Erin and Jessica were very young, their father, Scott, suggested that they learn from home. Every day, they spent a specific amount of time learning individual subjects according to traditional lesson plans. Their dining room became a school classroom. But then Scott realised that the girls were more excited about learning when they chose what to study and how to study it, so they started "unschooling".

It's All About Choices

Erin explains, "Every year before school started, we would choose books or subjects that we wanted to learn about. Of course there were the basics – English, maths and science – but everything else was our choice. There were topics that we would just get books and information about at our local library."

Scott says, "I became more relaxed and less concerned about keeping records and grading. I realised my daughters were learning all the time, and they loved to learn. They would set their own goals and finish them. In the end, my children were more than prepared for public school and life."

The Grand Oaks Academy

Erin and her sister, Jessica, did lots of their studying at their kitchen table, but that wasn't ideal. They had to keep moving their books whenever it was time for a meal. When Jessica saw plans in a woodworking book for a tree house, she knew she'd hit on a solution. They could "go to school" in a tree house in their own back garden!

Four months later, the tree house, called Grand Oaks Academy, was up and running. The tree house had heat and electricity, so the girls could have a computer in it.

My name is Erin, and I was unschooled until high school.

I would wake up around 7:30 and my dad would leave whatever schoolwork and chores I had to do that day on a note for me. When I was finished I had the rest of the day to do whatever I wanted. Most of the time, I would stretch out all my subjects over a week so I was done by lunch. I liked having time to go outside and just be a little kid.

Every other Thursday, I also went to a homeschool co-op called STAR and had different classes with other kids. Sometimes we just hung out. At STAR, I had a few more teachers.

Unschooling opened up so many possibilities for me. I was able to go to a quilting group and dance classes, volunteer at an 1850s living history farm and help my mom and dad with their work. My mom worked for a wildlife refuge, and my dad builds frames for houses.

Every year, my mom had to submit my grades to Gateway, an official homeschooling programme. We didn't really have tests or anything like that. So we would combine the studies that I was doing at home and the classes that I took at STAR and estimate a grade.

Fact: About 60,000 students in Canada and more than a million in the United States are homeschooled.

Off to School, Everyone

This book tells the stories of some incredible schools and the amazing people and students who make them work. And there are countless more stories waiting to be told. But even though there are amazing schools like these reaching out to children in every kind of situation, millions of others are still being left out. It's up to all of us to make sure they get a chance at an education, too. We need to keep asking, "What kind of schools do we need to create so these children, living here in these conditions, can learn?"

Hope Is Contagious

Telling stories about amazing schools and students is one small step that can help. Why? Because finding out that these incredible schools do exist, and that these children are learning, gives us hope – hope that even more schools can be created and even more children will get to go to school.

Hope is contagious, and it can turn into action. It inspires others to help. They may donate money. They may volunteer their time. They may talk to others in their community to change attitudes, or they may use their votes to change their government's policies. The more people get involved, the more children will get the chance to go to school.

Education is a basic human right. Spread the word. Keep hope alive. Turn it into action. And one day soon, every child everywhere in the world may get to go to school.

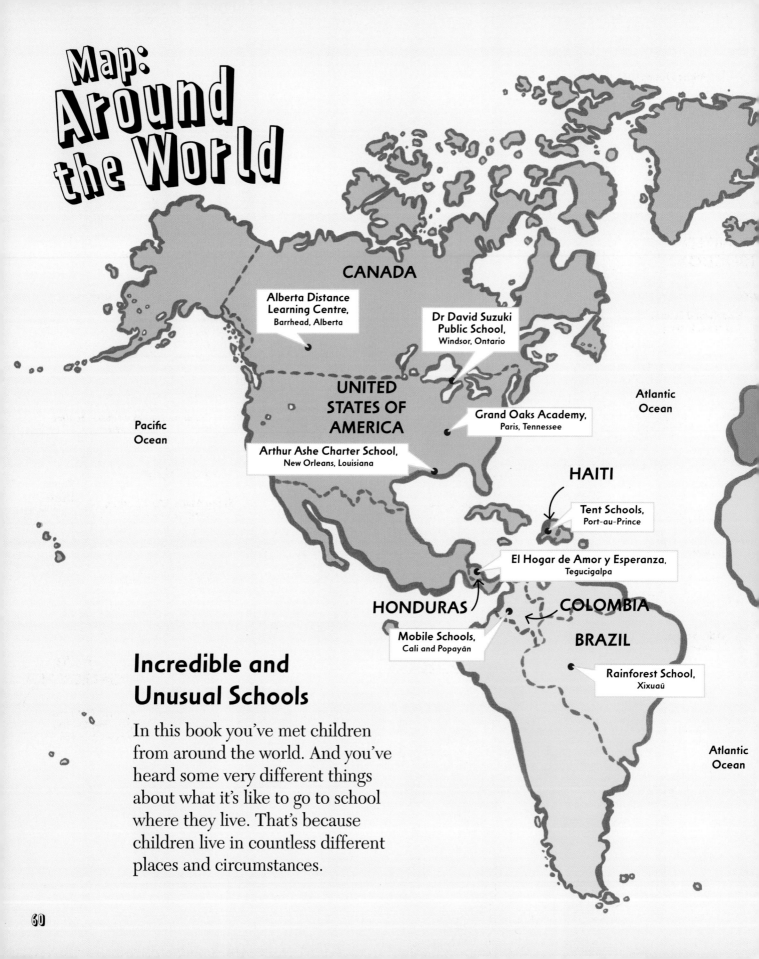

Map: Around the World

CANADA

Alberta Distance Learning Centre, **Barrhead, Alberta**

Dr David Suzuki Public School, **Windsor, Ontario**

UNITED STATES OF AMERICA

Atlantic Ocean

Pacific Ocean

Grand Oaks Academy, **Paris, Tennessee**

Arthur Ashe Charter School, **New Orleans, Louisiana**

HAITI

Tent Schools, **Port-au-Prince**

El Hogar de Amor y Esperanza, **Tegucigalpa**

HONDURAS

COLOMBIA

BRAZIL

Mobile Schools, **Cali and Popayán**

Rainforest School, **Xixuaü**

Atlantic Ocean

Incredible and Unusual Schools

In this book you've met children from around the world. And you've heard some very different things about what it's like to go to school where they live. That's because children live in countless different places and circumstances.

Arctic Ocean

**UNITED
KINGDOM**

Hazelwood School
Glasgow, Scotland

RUSSIA

Evenk Nomadic School,
Siberia

Shree Santi School,
Ramche

Druk White
Lotus School,
Shey

Beldangi-II Refugee Camp,
Jhapa District

BHUTAN

CHINA

NEPAL

IRAN

Door Step School,
Mumbai

Boat Schools,
Chalanbeel region

Dongzhong Primary School,
Dongzhong

Shahid Rajaei
Elementary School,
Kalou

INDIA

Portable Schools,
Bangkok

CAMBODIA

BURKINA FASO

Door Step School,
Pune

Stung Mean Chey Center,
Phnom Penh

THAILAND

Pacific
Ocean

Gando Primary School,
Gando

KENYA

UGANDA

Naning'oi Girls Boarding School,
Mosiro

ABC School,
Mutundwe

**NEW
CALEDONIA**

Indian Ocean

Alberta Distance
Learning Centre,
Virtual School, Kone

Resources

Interested in helping more children go to school?
Read on for information about how you can get involved.

Organisations

African Rural Schools Foundation
www.africanruralschools.org
Provides affordable schools for disadvantaged children in rural areas and emotional support for students who are affected or orphaned by HIV/AIDS.

Center for Architecture and Human Rights
www.architecture-humanrights.org
Promotes a rights-based approach to development in the practice of architecture, planning and engineering. Designed the portable school for the children of migrant workers in Thailand.

ChildFund International
www.childfund.org
Helps fund projects, like the Naning'oi Girls Boarding School, in developing countries.

Door Step School
www.doorstepschool.org
Runs a number of programmes for children in addition to the Schools-on-Wheels, including classes on pavements and classes at construction sites for children of labourers. Also runs a programme called Project Grow with Books for improving reading skills in schoolchildren.

El Hogar Projects
www.elhogar.org
Helps children in Honduras get off the streets and have a chance at a successful future through education.

Mobile School
www.mobileschool.org
Provides portable school kits for street educators around the world.

People Improvement Organization
www.peopleimprovement.org
PIO serves over 800 children a day in Cambodia through a variety of programmes that include non-formal education and vocational training.

Ruchika Social Services Organisation
www.ruchika.org
Dedicated to advancing the opportunities of under-privileged children in India through educational programmes, like the platform schools. Provides basic literacy, non-formal education, vocational training, nutrition, medical treatment and emergency assistance.

Shidhulai Swanirvar Sangstha
www.shidhulai.org
Works to improve quality of life in northern Bangladesh by taking services like schools and libraries to people by boat.

Solar Electric Light Fund
www.self.org
Empowers people in developing countries to escape from poverty using energy from the Sun.

UNICEF
www.unicef.org
As part of its worldwide humanitarian programmes, UNICEF provides schools-in-a-box for children affected by natural disasters.

Schools

Arthur Ashe Charter School
www.ashecharterschool.org
The Arthur Ashe Charter School is helping rebuild children's lives in the wake of Hurricane Katrina.

Dr David Suzuki Public School
www.suzukipublicschool.ca
Read more about the eco-friendly innovations in place at this remarkable school.

Druk White Lotus School
www.dwls.org
Discover how this unique school is helping preserve cultural traditions in its remote location.

Hazelwood School for Children and Young People with Sensory Impairment
www.hazelwood.glasgow.sch.uk
The innovations in place at this school will help sensory-impared children learn how to become independent adults.

Kalou School
www.dayyertashbad2.blogfa.com
This little school is having a big impact in its small coastal village in Iran.

Shree Santi School
www.santischool.org
This school is helping to break down the social stigmas that exist in Nepal's centuries-old caste system.

Acknowledgments

There are many people around the world who helped with the creation of this book. Most important are all those students – from Brazil to Uganda, Iran to New Caledonia – who agreed to contribute their thoughts and feelings about their schools. Thank you very much to Afsaneh, Anita, Arvin, Cameron, Eiann, Erin and Jessica, Eva, Hamideh, Hávar, Husnia, Jerome, Kaiya, Katarina, Laura, Madan, Mecias, Oona, Pariseh, Sophia, Sophie, Sukra, Tae Yoon, Tuqqaasi, Virginia, Xiao and Yordi. I only wish there were more pages in this book for sharing each one of your experiences!

I am grateful to the parents, guardians, teachers, principals and sponsors who provided me with information, connected me with others and supported the children in their responses. My many thanks to Ellen Armstrong, Marcel Braitstein, Graeme Bristol, Arnold Canlas, Elizabeth Canlas, Chris Clark, Annie-Claude Dupuy, Carolyn Freeman, Lila Jung Gurung, Bulime Hanan, Lona Hankins, Ann Van Hellemont, Chris Heun, Beth Hunt, Anuja Khemka, Gisèle Lautram, Gillian Lee, Sue Lendrum, Kara Lozier, Jennifer Meeker, Margo Mingay, Karen Nakamura, Phymean Noun, Darlene Nuqingaq, Mohammed Rezwan, Lynne Rickards, Lianne Roy, Gunnar Salvarsson, Shahla Sharifi, Abdul-Muhammad She'rani, Scott Stevens, Fred Teolis, Stu Thomas, Renee Waun, Amy Wei, Judy Wherry, Heli Ylinen and Kyongmi Yoo.

As well, I am greatly appreciative to Sheba Meland, Mary Beth Leatherdale, Larissa Byj and especially to my editor, Niki Walker, who saw the potential in my manuscript, shared my dream and helped define its focus. With much hard work and dedication, they helped to shape into one cohesive narrative a sprawling manuscript overflowing with stories about amazing schools around the world, the remarkable children for whom they were created and the inspirational citizens creating them.

Index

Article 28 of the United Nations' Convention on the Rights of the Child states that **every child has the right to an education.**

The UN developed a set of Millennium Development Goals to achieve by 2015. One of them is to **provide all children with a primary education, no matter where they live or how they live.**